Published by Flowerpublishing
©2018 Kevin Scott Josephs
ISBN 978-1-927914-85-4
All rights reserved. No part of this book may be reproduced, stored in a retrieval system or transmitted in any form or by any means without the prior written permission of the publisher, except by a reviewer who may quote brief passages in a review to be printed in a newspaper, magazine or journal

Flowerpublishing

www.flowerpublish.com

Montreal Canada

    improvisation.   Love as circumstance.
                    misfit.
Guts splayed & floored.   Bullets riddling dreamstate.
    Performance.   Arched bodies, tumbling into
              Secret chamber.
  Smoking to the light.
                    The feeling of face on granite.

                 Home.

Honor and Metaphor.   Illusion & nature
                  breathing.

You,
my perfect circumstance.

  Risk. Fingertips scolding. Hunger.   Repeat

a pulsing machine.

the affect is speaking

the Buried, have been tasked with   Beginning.
                with excavating and finding a new, Again

PROCESSIONS

by Kevin Scott Josephs

Illustrations by Lalo Remes

Contents, In Acts

I.   Of Knitted Things   pg 1

II. Floodlights   pg 45

III. Reflections, Part 1   pg 55

IV. Prayers: Affect Theory   pg 87

V.   August   pg 105

for,
  on,

     how we dream

I. Of Knitted Things

The rising tide.

We lived in a daze

and we live on a myriad of wondrous,
and ponderous   speculation
of my best case scenario.

The bumps,   in this long,
thunderous road
make the mornings in this reverie possible

and the resolution in form of:
locked limbs,
lips,
and head   to your chest,
makes the nights in this reverie

mine

September 5th

remember us as fading logic

You were the answer, I was the mark of a man who would not ask.
because I was sure love exists like this.   knowing and not knowing were only a matter of

time

I lived beneath us.
How could he not see?

how could he not welcomly embody all of our creation and what we would make it be?

                                                  remember , that we are

Gated Community

Youth.

The stubble grown through contrition Razor wire throat sprouting words that are foreign
That are around its topic of choice

But with depth that demands patience   Eyes that are in race… in doubt,

in love with this creature

Was raised in fire, I was made to burn like this.
His image imposed   on the foreground of every
            future - that's now taking precedent - over my memory

it has been this way, without my permission.

Why fight this?
what   would be the reason?

1:
his mind goes elsewhere. Like clockwork. Like, too much salt

Thinking up a perfect home:
his chair,

a wife,

those who allow his legacy to carry.   a blender

His calling that can make this destiny - this given - not only worth it,
but one that will make him willing

Taking credit for a future that was already written
Just feeling its glory.

      I sit on my hands.   Keeping them busy.

Try to fortify the fibers I have stitched around my pulse

Even if my heart is heaving itself in his direction - my arms lay against me.

Unchiseled stone
with no words
to be said,
to make us meet

      off of this conveyor belt
        leading to the slow burn of picket fence

...I want him
               wholly.

My sentences are beside themselves
: Jumbled
because my blood,
is outside itself

Rushing towards a destination it did not tell me it had in its plans.
Deserting me.

  ...maybe
  but leaving me the option to stand in its place

                                      (what a waste, this body has become)

     ...

... In a world - I imagine it is fighting for -
it would reach him,
burrow itself under skin
and be on its way to killing
him and I

              It would have us holy

plucked out of time
and release us from the obligations that this world provides

and let entropy have its way with us - as it must.

That,
would be our union

                                                                But,

2:

To feel the fury of a destiny.

To be at the peripheral of a vision
you need to see you complete

The heat arising
from effort
from trying to transpose the point of focus

    from: the comfort of that slow burn. The warm, feathery substance of euthanasia

    to: the armageddon
          made soft in your arms

                is unbearable in the body.

Fever of malnourished tongue leaves limbs hanging, and ached.
    Flaunting their mortal for a savior.

A savior, that they need to be now,
    but can't even find their way to his attention.

I have (to offer):

a) the melting of layers

b) the collision of bone at full speed

c) the need for sacrifice,
　the pull to kneel,
　with head bowed - in waiting
　can be accompanied by me

　　　　　and lastly

d) the congealing of body and grace
　　that will do what it must
　　　　to be

　　　the both of us.

　　　… I have
　　　　　　- to offer -
　　　　　　　　my hand

　　　　　　　　　　　　the whole way.

Compiling these gifts, on the desk next to his bed, I tally: one, set of arms,

with hands not enough....

3:		I wonder,		if he'll pray with me

if you have found what you seek,
if we both seek what we have found

then here and there we are, alone on my behalf, do we praise what we do keep

do we say: amen?

amen?

<u>Stencils</u>

> *You turned my scars into constellations*
> *making connections from one unthinkable sight to the next.*
>
> *You turned my space, into space,*
> *worthy of an ontology…*
>
> *or maybe just… a mythology*
>
>
> *that only heroes*
>   *could be written in to*

inscribe me.

please

September 28th

<u>Shards</u>

Wanting is such a delirious obsession
Holes wielded as reason for your necessity

Please, take control of me

Enter into this terrible fucking space that I lay

And hold

Me complete

I've been taking pictures in the mirror again.

Like what I see
or not,

a realignment would only think positively of me

<u>As You Will</u>

I want you

    to mark me   scar me   if

you will have me

If that is your only way to connect: to cut your way through
                                    what keeps you from being in us,

then bleed me.

Blood
  is thicker than romance.

I will bear your indictment   I am going   nowhere
without this   I will be ghost   in our home

I will love.

you have

my attention

i don't want you   to unhand it. give it back

it grows old with you,   let it whither in the comfort
of being held so close

Folklore

… you looked at me like murder,
like shame.

I wanted you to look. again,
and again

I wanted you to have empathy for my need
I needed you to feel me,
through skin,
through everything.

Leave your tracks on my corporeal gesture,
on me and this earth
so you'd have one to come back to.

Color me the back roads of your ephemeral.

A home that bled   not as sacrifice

                    but as calling

brittle crumbs

1

surface upon surface

skin   pushing
past
the thought
of another

sweat pouring   *into infinity*

2

…shades of ambrosia

…coiling limbs

…anything but unwind.

…loud indulgences
        slip, into the still walls of reality

…penetrate frontiers as

        bodies shatter.

3

corporeal angst

...

corporeal pleasure

we are the embattled blue of night

any night   can have its day

November 1st

Parcel and Substance

A picture frame,
punctured by wishful thinking of two mortals
praying about static.

Three
plastic
containers
atop a carpet of scattered crumbs.
The solace in batter

Only one
dangling from that keychain

Don't remember
that many locked places prior.

When I imagined this place   I thought of layers,
                              of traces,
                              that played witness
                              still – after we had been.

But quick and thorough.   forgetfulness.
 (palpable space. empty. thick.)

Just many walls. ceilings. floor.

And a whole that I wished would be more partial now that...

    just wishing there was a hole

Stop. *Watch.*

They are rising and... I wish for more hands, for her.
There is raising elbows, rolling shoulders, outstretched tips moving towards that part of infinity that lays right before... her ceiling.
Her motion, isn't meant for the morning. and she wouldn't ask her sight to direct this.

She just arcs bone, muscle, and finally, skin to a sky that is more crowded than she knew, to test, to be sure she still occupied this space.

This   voluptuous time-scape this   delicate portrait that   doesn't need language   to be.

A silhouette photographs her immediate   seamless   dance with sun

Until an unsentimental body leans   motioning a still life
   leaving one arm   laying off a bedside

Chipped and painted nails - worn, beautiful, threat, at rest

   extend from a sense.   one that   waits   to be kissed.

   I wish, for her, these hands.

                                                                                    Stop.

A high pile of books. Prim condition. Gigantically placed scribble on miniscule post-its.

   A speaker empty of notes.   Phone - dead - on the hook.

          Comb. Extension (cord). Anti(perspirant).

Nearly drawn (blinds).   Smoke (detector).   Still, damp, umbrella. (Hand) sanitizer.

       And a (not-locked) lock, on a closing (door). I wish it be jarred by,

                                        for,

                                                    because

                                                    remember me.

I just
came

to say

hello
 again…

I know. I do know. I'm not not listening I hear you

                                                                but

                                                                                us

<u>Rites</u>

      my eloquent behavior

          on tight rope   and dancing in the dark

      you can admit that you mirror me.   I will be waiting here, suspended

              for you to know that you want

II. Floodlights

December 31st

<u>Coliseum</u>

    The rains fall tired.

    Eyelids – dead,
        pristine as its sights

    The music box walks in reverse
        but secrets cling to corners like tips were molded for clench.

    Bottom rung exhibitionist
    pose and disfigure their figures
    for the taste they are needing to leave on the tongue of the wild.

    The ones with salivating eyes
        boundless hunger,

                phantom

                food

                for thought

do you ever starve as you feed?
                it's like being lungs without man to heed

                                  canister that is pure function, and more
doubt

I promised to never question path to our tomorrow
but love,

I am so hungry
without

Confession

In my most intimate sentiments
lay intimate benefits of:
knife to throat, throat to back of neck,
neck wrapped against chest of lover – intruder –

but grow calm as your memory fades into: black houses, white stones,
sad men, low roam.

Luckily, mass trajectory never effected

… or

never noticed how deep swords pinch
Bruise and spine running places I didn't even know
access could be.

Existing was out of question
in mind
no blessed coming – just heading
to waters.

Hadn't noticed that floods leave their epithets,
but not before epithets crystalize into midnight.

I keep asking,

Why won't dawns
end their becoming

    and become?

<u>Rorschach. or Hope</u>

lay knife against calm black stones
low trajectory.

running. didn't even know

question floods

but not:
midnight,
dawns
becoming.

and become

Ghosts

Labored,   laboring with plague of rage.

Body to hold it. No

        Sacraments of harmonizing blood – please – drift among rivers

        Say tomorrow like words among stars

        Say it cyclic: Transit conviction

        Say it, like it means

III. Reflections, Part 1

April 2nd

float
like dandelion

translucent.
holding breath

life teetering,

bodies bound to combust

and, to float

Rising Down

1
You dream magic.
I can see it in your stance that you're missing it
Have no recollection of it
but your body remembers.
Your hunger is for rain but you think in shelter
Your words can't ascertain the way your eyes do.

You are a beautiful movement

  The most beautiful movement.

      But the cage where you stay is fitted exactly for the size of someone you are not

you are used to

2
Hiding is for children

3
Escaping is for infants who will learn to stretch on their own behalf

I will not let you atrophy

i would build cathedrals
on the rumor of our name

brick upon brick
we could rhyme   the rhythm of our climbing to

what we've seen, how we've been, and
                              what God, has planned

then, they may hear us as   ascendant

then, may they come to see
what lays inside

                    stained glass,
                    and patience

Open Lanes

There is a blade that is held.

Its path imagined

            wrist
       along left center line

        to fold of elbow
        past scar,

    to shoulder,

    which is hunched
    and waiting for its fetal position to be loosened

                    and dropped.

to relax into a style of perfection

   where it had never been

This, is a glorious bastard.
From the womb of a mother
not his.

Not his spitting image of.

        Not his reflection   or his lineage.

No blood   but his   as proof   of him

        Blade to wrist

He had to make sure

that this exists

        they said:
to listen for own pulse

in arch of foot

rib cage

open letter

inner leg

in the person sitting across
your open wound

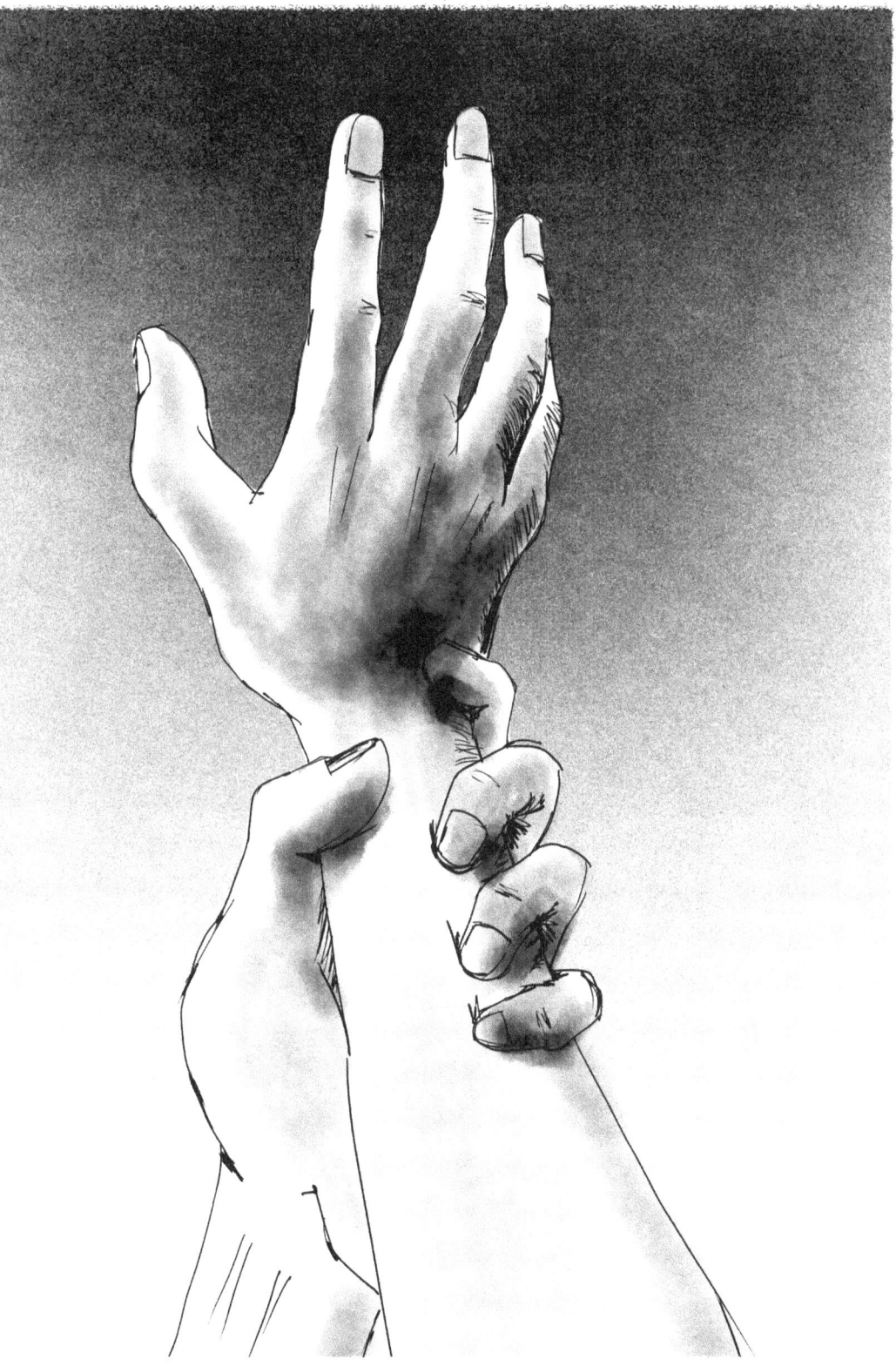

May 21st

<u>Grip</u>

Do you remember when we used to sleep in the daytime?

We swore that this solar powered engine we lived in was tired
way past its bedtime

And the moon   had so much to show,
too much to share
compared to the sparse amount of witnesses

Us and insomniacs   looking out the same windows.
Us and them   searching for what others take for granted.

You and me   holding on to nothing that we knew

In Brail

Hands,
were made

Left to float with their own vigor
and self-inflicted consequence

To intersect   for intrusion   and bleeding
                                     from going on boundary

Hands were made to be punished

so misstep,
insane?

So glory

1

Speaking of blood:

a heat   by way of tactless friction.

Curious ways made foolish   hungry.

Repetition
of lack strategy.

Forbiddance of thinking a man
The want   to feel.

Spine,
and bristle

Taking of no less.
Taking
of another's be unnoticed

Taking,

as fingers

would communion

2

And speaking of us:
                        you let me

Saw dream of man's thirst
and begged to see us as constellation.

Gave every day,   as sacrifice.

Put arms on bed to offer,

closed eyes,

felt us as one.

              Refused to understand   definition of a dream.

3

And speaking of me:
you slurred speech
until I had to:

come close,   come in,   block artery,

breath for two   and what we would make.

finally, hear you.

blow smoke so fire feel welcome

Break

1

Speaking of: warmth

        and of body:

This search for the light it hides
for the water it was birthed beside

will not know itself as 'blood' until

will not see itself as 'man' until

will not know you both as 'us' unless

                hands are used to unearth it

Llámame

    you, when were awoken
      by hand approached back.
    like the softest mistaken.

    And I wish you could have seen…
      the groove
    the spine made for a feel.

    A coiling.

    Prints,
    dissolving into figure
    Onto breath,

no reluctance of pleasure for a sense.

    We stand,

    fall,

      and intertwine

I am not shattered
in all places

       or for you

<u>Scythe</u>

I thought of rain often.   how it jumps to disappear.
how it collapses gentle on Earth, like it's the breath taken in

———

I could not recognize how we stood

like an embrace that knew what distinction was.did not want to remember.cried like it has

        memory.

    like it always would

———

these waters prepare themselves to dissolve in our salt, or to vaporate in our warmth.I know, by force or by time, the seeds that we've denied will be thanking us for this slim chance at sight,

whether they be drowned or with life.

        Our lungs need more than what we own

<u>Balaclava</u>

We danced – slowly

*You taught me how music
could be intrusive
to every single movement*

*that had to be picked out of the ethers
and preformed - not acted - together.*

We took baby steps, learning how to become one mind, by excusing both,

       flying blind.

Trancing now, vehicle of

    above-core left-center life-allowing

             pulse

IV. Prayers:
Affect Theory

reaching for prior.

having nightmares that cause
folding within, and on to itself

may it know the tenderness
of laying,
 palms facing down
in man and in earth,

repeat,
repeat upward turn

learning,   and considering

    a grace   that is yearned

Prints

I learned of bodies like God moved clay

The substance gave way to fingers,
caving to the want
of a curious,
(k)needing stranger.

And enjoying the true escape.

To be moved,
to be shifted along lines,
leading to destinations beyond guessing,
beyond hope,
is being a part of creation.

these limbs got to learn
that they were more

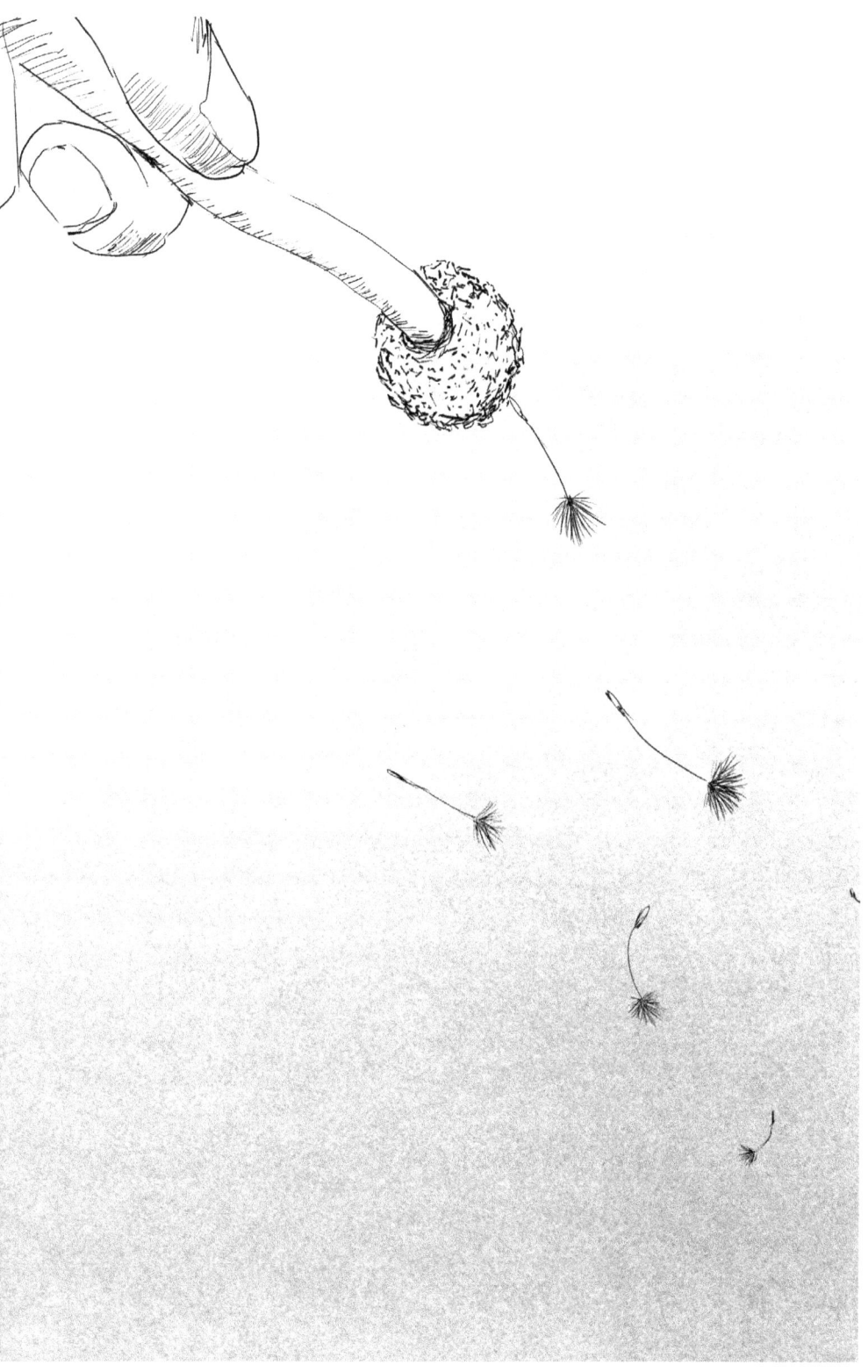

Cold, Dark Machine

Body has a motion.

The crease shown
when limbs are pulled apart
to reveal link
between

bottom,
and middle,
and top,
and outer, and blood

and knuckles grazing another's entire tapestry of light,

and tongue clawing to witness an interiority
trying to hold back the frustration
of not being able to bathe its entirety.

trying to resist the urge
   to bite.

the crease moves,
stretches,
attempting to allow full access
    (reverence for the pieces scattered)

leaving no corner
no crevice
no particle
    aside

A baptism.

why can't we...

May we all   come alive

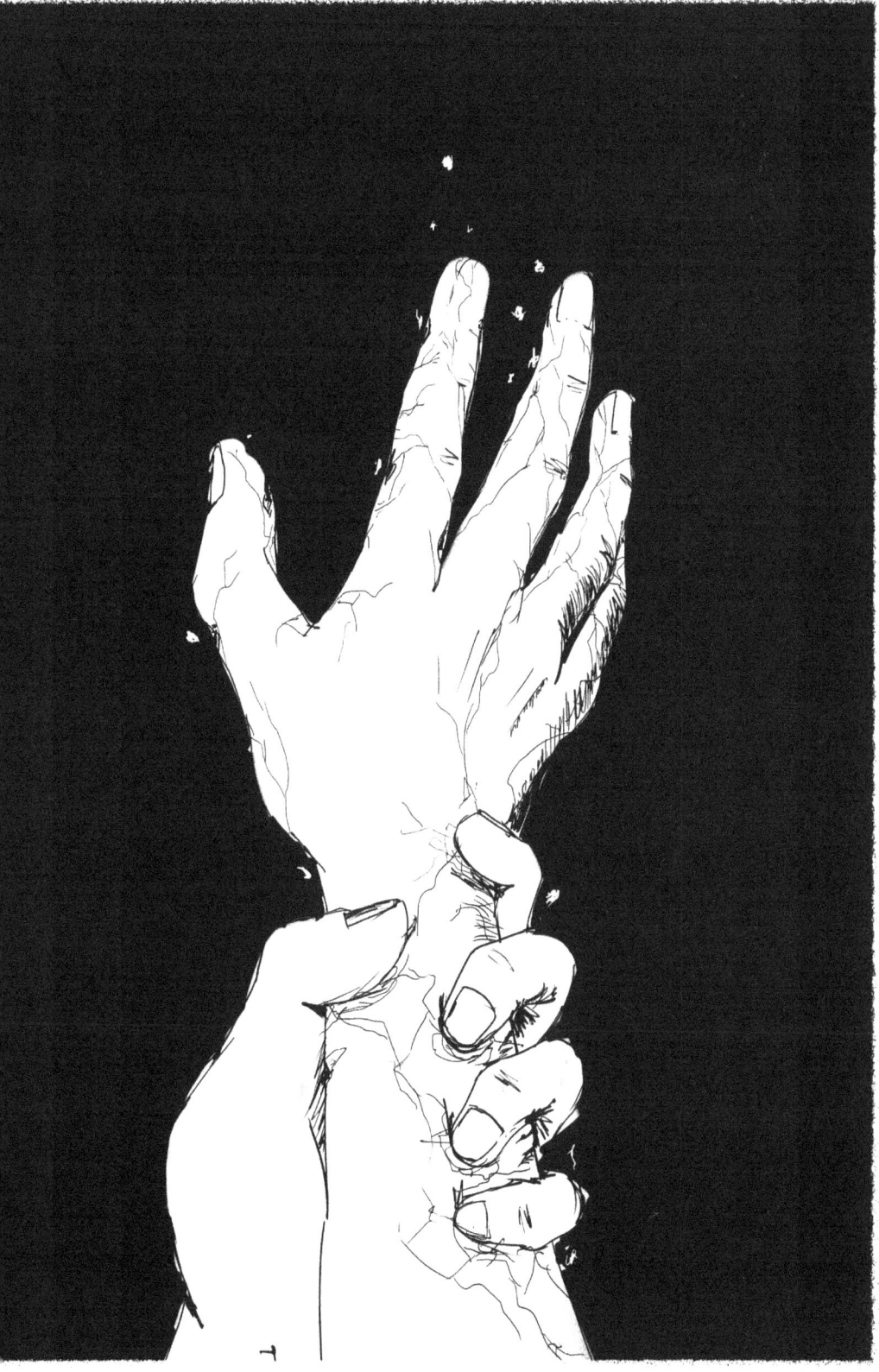

<u>shimmering.</u>　　<u>quaking.</u>　　　<u>dis.ease</u>

　　　　　　———

Sterling.
　Nuanced.
　　Changing

Shades of gray.

Of love secreted
　　　　　　in sweat.　heat.　Into beds　　unmade

Pure Affliction

A memory?
Taste buds   see salt.
They are embracing creases.

They are moving across marks that are proof that you stretched,
were reaching for something other than

Relax
Am here

Seeing textures of hair,
against battered layers of memory
You, with your pristine look of agony

Chewing   bone.
Naming sweat

Dying to feast on what is inside
 teeth crave the impossible

You, the beauty that you are,
dig deeper
and bring pulse to memory.

    You   let me taste tears   instead

<u>devout</u>

you let me
 I: allowed you
     was allowed to
     give thanks, because I do not know how to give praise

a man   was the same calling I had for you
                                            in vain

with sympathy, please: forgive me

I am learning that we – the end and beginning of call and receive
are not one, or either.

we are

                                                                   .a men

V. August

at bloom

Timing is anything

                                      he was a masked avenger, filled with a heading, of I,
                                                                            f all this angst

world turns slower as the end is reached

                        and I battled, and tried to kill the only thing that mattered to him…
                                                                                               covered in blood

the way out is through the center, through the eye, as it weeps

                                      but he kept close, to catch the shattering of my arms
                                  when bearing was overcome by a memory, informing me,
                                that glass was bound to hatch if I attempted to reach

it rains when the levies break, when the sky is torn, for us to be considered forewarned that waters are only still, for a time

        I pushed back against, wanting to fall through the shadow of my manic haze. but he was solid, and branded him, and I, as a minor fate. Microcosm for whole

the lights that the morning cast, were patient with their pitch for new day come, waiting for eyes and withered palms, to hear

        hastening his pace, he jettisoned his focus for his ear, to this face, wondering how scents get locked away behind a tone that can lie.

        never good enough

the night has won, even with achy silence and wanting as heir. the now,
the lacking object explodes into morsels of could not hear, speak, doubt, think
and the ones left to feel, are in awe

a subtle face, and an empty wound
lay dormant as I - who is sure to be dead soon –
halts, and wavers that destined to fall
into skin so abrupt.   Unconvinced.now.
Wanting to test unfamiliar... my luck

the question of burning is not the thought of fire,
but one of ash. and newly grown leaves;

naked. Like fruit picked from orchard,
by witness, interest peaked. He told me,
that we were made for nowhere. that he would take me from

the black slow, of blazed snow
brings fallen into focus

                        with hollow bone that he left for favor, I am marked.
                        We – the passing embrace of time, and lifted.ness.
                        I gave him my soul, on platter, to feast.
                        No need for what lies, has laid, underneath.
                        I've tasted every surface that matters,
            and he, is intimate, familiar with skin that is scoured with

                                        a trembling.   a sin

that ice,
that tough,
that cool,
that slick.

this feel
is omnipresent

                                               we: shake, loud, aches.
                                    a birth, is more than destine

As the stars turn, with rumor of distance, a rigid water marks blooms of capacity met and overtaken by a pulling of sun to moon, god to you. for night will have its day. in place of some far off calling from the panic of voices that are disembodied, and men, in vain...

                            And the sweet, and the sweat,
                       has disappeared and we are left,
                          roaming with hands – our gaze.
            And i'll say: god has come to this place, and left.
          Trusting its sons with the rigid water they have lent,
                                    and given away,
                                  and gotten back.

        I'll say:
                body is a wretched,
                an imperfect,
                is a bless-ed.

        Body.
        the place

                    we will stay

aman.

When Woke

The rising tide.

We switch positions in the future, in a memory. And we both end up being in about the same place that we started individually.

So… what is individuality?   What is it anymore?

You hoist your world up on your shoulders,
    next to a man with fallen dreams, and you see to it

that neither could even think, to hit the bottom of a trajectory.

        Suspended.

I   hook arm   within someone else's,
bringing heat, from cold and distant places.

Being close enough, where distinctions can't be met   or   made.

    You spoke of a void, but

clawing out of skin

        entering into yours

God

I am beautiful

September 5th

Interlude

Leg above shoulder.
Above ladders.

Beneath heaven.

                right
                  next to a morning.

Sun plays
on torso as lust

bobs
and weaves
its way
to a center.

A temple?

                        a body:

                        scoured of light

www.ingramcontent.com/pod-product-compliance
Lightning Source LLC
LaVergne TN
LVHW091307080426
835510LV00007B/402